# Hamster

## Care

T.F.H. Publications
One TFH Plaza
Third and Union Avenues
Neptune City, NJ 07753

This book has been published with the intent to provide accurate and authoritative information in regard to the subject matter within. While every precaution has been taken in preparation of this book, the publisher and author assume no responsibility for errors or omissions. Neither is any liability assumed for damages resulting from the use of the information herein.

ISBN 0-7938-1026-4

www.tfh.com

# Table of Contents

# You & Your Hamster

Each person chooses a pet for different reasons. Some animals are chosen for the companionship they provide, some for convenience, and some because they are simply adorable. The hamster fits into all three categories. Hamsters are popular pets for many reasons. They are quiet, almost odorless, and have cute facial expressions. They are easy to care for in respect to housing and food and come in an extensive range of colors and patterns. Once hamsters are hand tamed, they become very friendly little pets. Hamsters are inexpensive to purchase, easy to care for, do not take up a lot of space, and don't create any disturbance or make much of a mess. In addition to all these wonderful qualities, they are lovable, cuddly, and endearing.

# Hamster Antics

Hamsters do a lot of interesting and amusing things, one of which is hoarding food in their cheek pouches. The hamster, whose name comes from the German word *hamstern*, which means "to hoard," stuffs food into his pouches until he looks like a trumpet player practicing his musical art. After he has filled his cheek pouches (which stretch and expand like a balloon), he scurries away to hide his treasure, often underneath his mattress of natural wood shavings.

Hamsters can provide hours of entertainment and merely require loving care and attention from their owners.

Hamsters usually play in the evening or night, because they are nocturnal creatures and have adapted their senses to help them move around in the dark. Some hamster owners have devoted entire rooms in their homes to their hamsters. They set up elaborate hamster playgrounds complete with exercise wheels, slides, ladders, rides, and other sources of amusement for both the hamster and the hamster owner.

## Variety

Some people like hamsters because of the interesting variety of coat colors that are available. Originally introduced to the pet scene and to pet lovers as the Golden or Syrian hamster, these little animals have been bred in countless other colors. Today, there are white hamsters, black hamsters, panda hamsters, Teddy Bear hamsters and many other color variations. Chinese and Dwarf hamsters, from other regions of the world, are also available and popular pets today.

Quick & Easy Hamster Care

If hamsters are treated kindly and given a comfortable, roomy cage that is kept clean, they are gentle and responsive pets. And as any pet owner knows, you get from a pet what you give to that pet.

Hamsters are social creatures that like to play and love to be handled. You should not simply put a hamster in a cage and forget about him. You should want to make friends and socialize with your pets. This means handling them. Hamsters like to play and they like you to play with them. After a while, they start to recognize your voice and will even sit up on their hind legs and listen when you talk to them, especially if you happen to have a tasty hamster treat in your hand!

*Hamsters are friendly pets that provide hours of enjoyment for people of all ages.*

*Golden hamsters originate from the deserts of the Middle East. They are commonly found in hobbyist's homes throughout the world.*

## Hamster History

The Golden hamster is but one of 24 species of hamster that are found in the Old World from Europe to Asia and China. It was first imported into England during the 19th century. The stock seems to have died out around 1910 without having created any great impact.

Professor I. Aharoni of the Department of Zoology at Hebrew University in Jerusalem is considered the "father" of the pet hamster. In 1930 the professor was out in the field near Aleppo, Syria, when he found a mother hamster and her litter. The professor took this family back to the university where the hamsters were bred and became the source of pet Golden hamsters today.

A year after the professor's discovery, descendants of these hamsters were shipped to England, where they were sent to commercial breeders, a university, and the London Zoo.

Quick & Easy Hamster Care

In 1938, several hamsters were sent to the United States, but this cute little mammal did not really make any great impact on the pet world until the late 1940s and early 1950s. It then took off in a big way and has remained extremely popular ever since. In 1971, a small group of these animals was imported into the US, possibly the first fresh bloodlines since the original captives of 1930.

## Hamsters in Nature

The hamster is a small mammal about five inches long (13cm) that weighs approximately four ounces (115g). The female is usually somewhat larger and heavier than the male. However, this is a relative matter, and is not the basis for sex determination. The tail is short, about half an inch (1.5cm) in length. Hamsters live solitary lives in small burrows and are basically nocturnal, but may venture forth during daylight hours.

Before the hamster became a pet, the many varieties existed in several exotic and demanding environments. Golden hamsters,

*Hamsters are quiet, clean pets that are easy to care for and come in a variety of colors.*

for example, come from the desert of the Middle East, where the temperature range is extreme and where the amount of water available is minimal.

To survive in the hot climate, the Syrian hamster sleeps underground in a cool burrow during the day. He goes out at night for food, seeds, insects, and whatever desert greenery is available. Sometimes food is not readily available, and for this reason, nature has endowed the hamster with stretchable cheek pouches to carry and store food.

Chinese and Dwarf hamsters, from the northern regions of Asia, live in an almost entirely different world than their southern cousins. While the Syrian hamster's world is dominated by heat, the Chinese and Dwarf hamsters' environment is usually cold. Snow and cold temperatures send these hamsters into hibernation deep underground. Because the summers are short and the winters are long, the Chinese and Dwarf hamsters, like squirrels, gather food in the fall, which they store until the short summer begins.

Hamsters are omnivorous, which means their diet consists of roots, plants, seeds, invertebrates, and any carrion that they discover as they forage. If the weather gets very cold, or food is scarce, hamsters will undergo a short hibernation of up to twenty-eight days. Some species will go into hibernation for just a few days, wake up to feed on their stored food, go back to sleep, and repeat the process. A hamster's life span averages a thousand days, but some may live somewhat longer if they have hibernated frequently.

In the following chapters, everything you need to know about housing, care, and generally enjoying these desirable little rodents is discussed.

# Housing Your Hamster

Experienced pet owners know just how important it is to be organized when it comes to taking care of animals. Things will always go more smoothly if you already have everything you need for your new hamster before you bring him home.

## The Right Cage

Hamster cages vary in size, but it is advisable to get the biggest cage you can afford. The bigger and roomier the cage, the more room you will have for food dishes, water bottles, and toys. Hamsters love to play, and their cage should allow them ample room to exercise and frolic. The hamster is a very active little creature who likes to do all kinds of acrobatic tricks. You should, in fact, encourage him to stay active and get this kind of exercise. A hamster that has been kept in a cage that is too small and that doesn't enable him to get the right amount of exercise can become nervous and snappish.

A cage that measures about 24 inches in length, 18 inches from front to back, and about 12 inches from top to bottom should be sizeable for your hamster.

 **Housing Essentials**

To get your hamster set up in his new home, you'll need:

- a proper cage (approximately 24 x 18 x 12 or larger)
- a nest box
- an exercise wheel and/or playground
- toys such as plastic tubes, blocks of wood or ladders
- bedding
- food and water dishes

When you bring your hamster home, allow him to get used to his new surroundings gradually. Place him in the cage with sufficient food and water and leave him alone for a while. Let him adapt to the place and in a day or two you can gradually start to get to know him a little better. Give your hamster time to adjust until he feels at home in his cage and with you. Any animal is going to be nervous in a new environment, especially if people are picking him up and putting him down. The atmosphere for a new pet should be on the tranquil side. He might be frightened by loud noises, such as slamming doors, loud music, the TV, or a lot of people hovering over him.

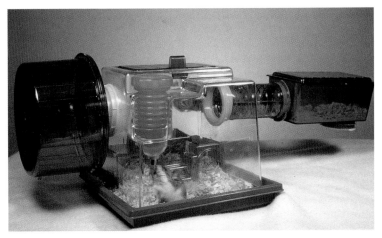

*Your hamster's cage should be easy to clean and contain space for him to exercise.*

## Cage Types and Care

Birdcages and fish tanks have been used as hamster housing, but these are not the best choice for hamsters. One argument against use of an aquarium tank for the hamster is the possibility of humidity build-up. A hamster's surroundings should always be kept dry and clean. The tank traps the hamster's body heat, which in turn generates humidity, especially if the air circulation in the tank is not good.

Cages should also be easy for you, as the hamster's principal housekeeper, to handle and clean. Many commercially manufactured cages are streamlined for easy handling, which is fine as long as they are sturdy enough to withstand the lifestyle of the hamster and the frequent house cleanings for which you will be responsible. It's always a good idea to go with a product that looks and feels a little on the sturdy side. In addition to your frequent cleanings of the cage, that cage is also going to be gnawed on by the hamster.

Most cages today are made of plastic and metal, preferable for a number of reasons. One is that hamsters will gnaw wood, which might fill the cage and the hamster's sensitive cheek pouches with

## The Single Life

splinters. Plastic and metal are also preferred to wood because wood absorbs urine and will create dampness in the cage. Certain cages are equipped with sliding trays made of plastic, glass or metal, to make it easier for you to clean.

The roof, or top of the hamster's cage should be secure and escape-proof. Hamsters are always looking for ways to get out of their cage and they know how to do it. Make sure the top of the cage and any other openings in the cage are secure.

While the cage roof and sides can be made of wire so the hamster can climb up the swing on the bars, the bottom of the cage should

*Aspen wood shavings is the preferred bedding material for hamsters. Line the bottom of the cage with about two to three inches of shavings, so your hamster can make a cozy bed from it.*

Quick & Easy Hamster Care

not have a wire or wire-grating surface. In addition to the wire being uncomfortable for the hamster to walk on, his tiny feet could become trapped or snagged in the wire.

## Cage Accessories

Some cages come complete with a small raised platform on which there is a nest box reached via a plastic tube or ladder. Other cages come without fittings, which you must provide. For the unfurnished cage, you should obtain a plastic nest box and an exercise wheel (the solid type rather than those with open metal or plastic treads). These items and other hamster cage accessories are available in a range of styles from any good pet shop. You can add a few items that your hamster will enjoy. A wooden bobbin is always of interest to your pet, as is a plastic tube in which he can scamper in and out of. A few large pebbles in one corner will provide something upon which he can clamber. One or two pieces of fruit tree branches will be useful for your pet to gnaw on and gain nutritious fibrous material in the process.

## Bedding

While the hamster's cage should be sturdily constructed of plastic, metal, and wire (no wood), the interior of the cage should be furnished with the hamster's need for comfort in mind. The cage should be deeply padded with aspen wood shavings or wood chips. *Never use cedar chips or shavings in the bedding of any small mammal.* Cedar contains phenols that can cause upper respiratory problems when inhaled. (Pine shavings also release compounds, but to a lesser

### A Cozy Bed

To make the best bed for your hamster's comfort and safety, choose aspen or wood shavings. Pile the shavings nice and deep for burrowing, and keep it clean!

degree.) The bedding should be spread out over the bottom surface of the cage to a depth of one to two inches. Hamsters sleep and hoard food in one area of their cage using these materials. They also use these same materials in another part of their cage for their toilet.

Your hamster will appreciate it if you provide extra layers of bedding in the sleeping area. The hamster will burrow down into it. Don't put pieces of cotton or old blankets or towels into the cage. The hamster will chew on them and probably ingest bits of cloth. This can be dangerous to your pet.

## Cage Location

It is important that you select the location for your pet's home with care. The cage should not be placed where it might be exposed to a draft, such as opposite a door. Nor should it be placed where it will be subject to the direct rays of the sun for any length of time. Likewise, do not place it over or near a radiator that is constantly going off and on. This will result in sudden temperature fluctuations that are not healthy for any pet.

The cage needs to be placed at a convenient height so that you can easily attend to cleaning chores without having to bend over. At the same time, you will more readily be able to watch your pet's activities if the cage is on a table or shelf.

Hamsters like temperatures that are a little on the warm side, preferably in the 65° to 72°F (18-22°C) range. If, however, you like things a little cooler, you should take extra steps to make the hamster's living area warmer. You might provide little more insulation and warmth by putting a blanket over the cage at night (remembering the need to maintain good air circulation) or by adding an extra layer of insulation underneath the hamster's cage.

You can also close the heating vents in your room or your side of the room while keeping them open in the hamster's room or the

*If your hamster becomes cold or bothered by bright light, he will burrow under his shavings to sleep where it is dark and warm.*

hamster's side of the room. In the summer, or during warm weather, keep your pet away from the air conditioner or air conditioning vents.

If the temperature in your home drops too low, your hamster may go into a state of hibernation. In hibernation, the hamster will sleep, the body gets rigid and the animal's body temperature drops. If this situation does occur, you can bring your pet out of hibernation by gradually turning up the heat.

The hamster's sensitivity to cold and to sunlight (his eyes weren't designed for exposure to bright light) are two reasons why the cage should be generously filled with wood shavings. If your hamster gets too much light or becomes too cold, he can always burrow deeper in the cage where it is darker and warmer.

## A Hamster's Playground

One reason why people like hamsters is the fact that they are

*Hamster toys and exercise equipment can be purchased from your local pet shop. Hamsters like to play with wheels, ladders, and plastic tunnels.*

entertaining little fellows who like to play. You can bring out his natural playfulness, and also help to satisfy his need for important exercise, by setting up a hamster playground.

The hamster playground can be as elaborate as you like, but it must include an exercise wheel. Not only is it fun for the hamster to run on, but it will provide a good way for him to get the right amount of exercise he needs. This need for exercise cannot be emphasized enough. Without enough of it, a hamster can fall victim to a form of cage paralysis.

Many commercially designed playgrounds are available in most pet stores. You can start with the basics and keep adding on, similar to adding new pieces to an electric train system. There are wheel rides for hamsters, pet houses, ladders, slides, revolving wheels, and stairways to upper floors for the hamster to climb. Remember one thing, though: the more intricate and the more interesting some of this may be, the more difficult it will be to clean and to keep clean.

While the hamster is sure to use these and other toys, don't force him to. He should play because he wants to play, not because you want him to.

The commercial manufacturers of hamster equipment have certainly covered most of the bases when it comes to the hamster playground. But those who are handy or who like to provide the homemade touch can also use books, pipes, tubes, and other props found around the home to create still other diversions for their pets. Hamsters like to play in and hide in mazes and caves. You can also fill up a box of wood shavings for them to burrow, hide, and sleep in.

Remember to keep safety in mind if you do choose to construct some homemade hamster toys or hide-a-ways, and be certain that everything you put into the cage is secure and won't come tumbling

## Quick & Easy Cage Cleaning

To keep your hamster happy and healthy, follow this basic routine.

Every day:
- wash food containers
- fill the food dish with pellets
- remove any hoarded food that appears moldy
- rinse and refill the water bottle

Each week:
- remove all bedding
- scrub out the cage and accessories
- wash and dry all toys and exercise equipment
- wash out the water bottle
- replace the bedding

down. Make sure tunnels are wide and ladders won't fall. If you use heavier materials to create little nooks and crannies, make sure that these materials can't topple over.

## Routine Cleaning

One way to keep your hamster happy and healthy is to thoroughly clean his cage once a week. Just as you have to take care of the hamster and make sure that he gets the right food and enough drinking water, you will also have to be both maintenance person and housekeeper for his cage. While the hamster is naturally a clean animal, a cage is a man-made structure and needs human hands to attend to it. The words "clean" and "dry" should always be on your mind when it concerns the hamster's environment.

The hamster's droppings, normally dry and hard, are usually left in one area. Some hamster owners say that they find the animal's

*All hamsters need exercise every day. Exercise wheels should be constructed of plastic, not wire, to prevent the hamster's feet from getting sore or injured.*

Quick & Easy Hamster Care

# The Tube System

There are now a number of variations on this interesting method of housing hamsters. Basically, they comprise a number of tubes that are connected to large tub-like structures that are used as nests, toilets, and general eating areas. The great advantage of these systems is that you can start with a basic kit and then keep adding on. You can create a very interesting miniature tunnel system that equates to the home of the hamster in the wild. The tubes are made of clear plastic so that you can watch your pet as he moves around the series of tunnels and dens.

The only cautionary note with these tubes is that a large and overweight hamster just might get stuck occasionally! Do keep an eye on your pet as he travels through the tunnels so that you are sure he has no problems.

droppings all over the cage, but generally, the hamster will use one corner of his cage for his toilet and another corner for sleeping and hoarding. The toilet area should be cleaned out every day and new bedding should be added as needed. When you clean and remove old shavings, always be sure to put enough new shavings back into the cage.

While the toilet area should be cleaned daily, the hamster's sleeping area should be cleaned and changed once or twice a week. Replace all the litter in the urinal area every two or three days.

You may want to set up a smaller "spare" or temporary cage for your hamster to live in while you are cleaning out his primary home. When cleaning the cage, remove and dispose of all floor covering and bedding material. Wash the cage base and the bars thoroughly, avoiding any substances that could be toxic to your pet. Rinse the bars and base well and allow them to dry completely before adding the clean floor covering and nest box material.

Food dishes and containers should be washed daily, and the water bottle should be filled daily and washed weekly. When you are cleaning the cage, look for any leftover food that might be hidden away or rotting. Clean that out immediately. Do not, however, disturb your hamster's hoard of dry pellets. If you upset his hoard, it is very likely you will also upset your hamster. Be sure to wash and dry the plastic play tunnels and all toys and exercise equipment once a week.

## Stay Home or Roam?

This is a question individual hamster owners, with different styles of handling pets, will have to answer for themselves. Some people are quite content to leave their pets in their cage at all times, never letting them out. Other hamster owners let their pets out to play with them or even set them on their laps to "watch" television.

*Your hamster's cage must be cleaned daily. Be sure to add new shavings to replace the soiled ones.*

If you are thinking of giving the hamster a little more room to run around in every now and then, please consider these factors: other animals in the house; small children in the house; open windows; and open doors.

Under the right conditions and with good supervision, the hamster can be let out of his cage. Don't let him out of his cage the day you bring him home, however. Wait until he gets the feel of your house and becomes familiar with you. Always start animals out with small areas, gradually expanding their territory.

You should limit the hamster to the exploration of one room. Close all windows. Make sure the door is closed and be certain that he won't be able to slip under the door. Seal off closets and air vents as well. And, of course, be there at all times, otherwise, he will soon disappear under a sofa, behind a heavy appliance, into a crack in your floorboards, or in some other equally difficult-to-get-at location. Needless to say, your hamster must never be allowed to roam free in a room that contains a cat or other household pet.

The best time to let your hamster run around is usually in the evening or when things have quieted down around your house. You

## Hamsters and Other Pets

Caution is the word when it comes to mixing hamsters and other pets. It can be done under very close and strict supervision. Yes, hamsters can make friends with dogs and cats, but you have to remember that these pets are much larger than the hamster and may see him as a toy or prey. Therefore, it's better for everyone involved not to put hamsters and other pets together.

In addition to keeping the animals apart, make sure that the hamster's cage is securely protected and positioned in the room so that these animals cannot claw through the bars or knock the entire cage over.

don't want people coming in and out, opening and shutting windows, slamming doors, and making a lot of noise. Let your hamster wander during a quiet time of the day when everything is relaxed.

Hamsters can damage things found around the house. They might chew electrical wires and extensions, or wires that hook up to stereos and speakers. Never give a hamster a chance to get near electric cords and other wiring, as this can create a dangerous situation for everyone. Your hamster may also nibble on objects that are not good for him, such as carpeting, books, clothing, or newspaper. Hamsters are small, they can get into upholstered furniture or disappear under a sofa or a chair. If you do let your hamster run free, remember he can climb and get into the unlikeliest of places. Keep a close eye on your pet.

## Escapes

Do all that you can do to prevent the hamster from escaping in the first place. See that his cage is secure, that the bars are not too wide. A hamster is always looking for ways to get in and out of things. But what if your hamster does escape? Whatever you do, don't conduct an unorganized, noisy search for him. This will frighten him and make him even more difficult to find.

The first thing you should do is to look everywhere you think he could possibly hide, such as under a sofa, in the upholstery of a sofa, or a chair. This is why it is a much better idea to keep the hamster, if you do let him out of the cage from time to time, confined to one room in your home. If that room is securely sealed, it will make your search for the missing hamster that much easier, you'll know that he has to be somewhere in that room. (Incidentally, you should make sure that this room doesn't have any loose boards or holes in the walls that the hamster can fit through.)

Should your hamster escape, don't panic! There are several tricks

*Hamsters are naturally curious pets. Be sure you have a secure lid on your hamster's cage to prevent escapes.*

Housing Your Hamster

you can try to get your hamster return home. Food is often very useful in helping an animal find his way back home. Try using a piece of carrot, sunflower seeds, or some of the hamster's favorite snacks to lure him back. Open the cage and fill the food dish with an extra supply of his favorite food. Leave the room and check from time to time to see if he has returned on his own.

Another option is to put some food in his cage and leave the cage (with the door open) near where you think the hamster is hiding. He may return to the cage for food and stay there because he might have been frightened while away. You may have to leave the cage open overnight.

A good trick to use is to place a small bucket in the room and line the base with a thick layer of shavings. Next, put some enticing edibles, such as pieces of apple and favored seeds, into the bucket. Now build a non-skid ramp and place a trail of tidbits far apart all the way up the ramp. With any luck, your hamster will follow the trail of goodies until he reaches the top of the bucket, where he may jump in to get at the main course. Once you have recaptured your hamster, be sure to keep a close eye on him and try to block off any escape routes or hiding places you may have discovered.

# Feeding Your Hamster

A hamster, like any other animal, needs a well-balanced diet with the right amount of vitamins, minerals, and other nutrients. Today, most commercially-prepared hamster foods contain most everything a hamster needs to stay healthy and active. Available in most pet stores, these nutritious dry food pellets should form the basis of your hamster's diet for this and two other important reasons: the pellets are easy to hoard, and gnawing on the pellets helps keep the hamster's ever-growing teeth from becoming too long.

Variety in a hamster's diet is important. One simple way to start developing some variety in your hamster's diet is to serve your pet hamster different types of pellets and basic hamster chow. There are many hamster treats, snacks, and other food supplements available in pet shops. You can also make your own hamster treats and snacks from foods available in your local grocery store.

Some hamster owners disagree over whether or not to provide fresh fruits and vegetables to their pets. If they are hoarded, they will spoil and bacteria will build up inside the cage. However, if you give them small bits at a time, the hamster won't get a chance to hoard anything where it might spoil.

A lot of hamsters like alfalfa, and you can purchase alfalfa treat squares, which are natural, but prepared. Consisting of 100% natural dehydrated alfalfa, alfalfa treats provide necessary fiber roughage, and the hard surfaces are also helpful in maintaining your hamster's teeth.

## Top Food Choices

Hamsters like a variety of foods, including:
Alfalfa, fresh fruits and vegetables (carrots, spinach, corn, grapes, and apples), seeds (sunflower, grain, oats), and fresh grass. Offer your hamster a variety – he will let you know what he likes!

*Commercially-prepared pelleted food contains all the necessary nutrients your hamster needs and should make up the majority of the hamster's diet.*

Because most of the commercially-prepared hamster food products contain certain amounts of vegetable ingredients, such as ground corn, soybean meal, alfalfa, ground oats, and other vegetables, some hamster owners are quite content to serve only these store-bought food products.

Others serve fresh vegetables to their hamsters. Recommended vegetables for hamsters include carrots, spinach, lettuce, and corn. Individual hamster tastes vary. Some hamster owners say that their pets like fruits such as apple slices, grapes, and bananas; others say not. Why not give your hamster a sampling of different foods to find out what he likes?

Be sure to wash thoroughly any fruits and vegetables that you are going to give to your hamster to eliminate any traces of pesticides or dirt that may be on the fresh food. Also, be sure to check the cage a

# Fresh is Best!

Always serve food that is fresh. While dry food won't spoil as quickly as fruits and vegetables, you should always check the age of the dry food by looking at the food processor's milling date on the box. Pellets, seeds, seed mixes, and other dry foods that have been around too long can go bad, and this "old" food can make your hamster sick. If dry foods are stored in damp locations, they can lose their crispness and become moldy. Always store these dry foods in a dry place and never feed your hamster anything that does not smell or look fresh.

few hours after these foods are served, so they do not remain hoarded, where they can spoil.

## Snacks and Treats

Besides being another source of food, hamster treats and snacks provide a number of useful functions. These snacks and treats come in all shapes and sizes, and one thing they do is add more variety to the animal's basic diet.

These commercially-prepared treats are usually in dry form and don't create any problems, such as spoilage, associated with perishable snacks.

Hamster snacks and treats also ensure that your pet gets all the nutrients he needs. Fiber roughage should be a part of your hamster's basic diet. If you are having trouble getting this for your pet, there are 100% natural dehydrated alfalfa treats that will provide it. There are also other combinations of dehydrated vegetables in the form of snacks or treats, some of which can be added to the hamster's regular food each day. There are even cheese-flavored hamster food supplements formulated to supply your pet with additional sources of protein.

Most pets like crunchy treats, and the hamster is no exception. Besides being tasty, they help to keep his teeth in good condition. Most crunchy treats and snacks also contain ingredients enriched with vitamins and minerals.

Whether they are in the form of squares or wafers, crispy sticks or cookies, hamster snacks and treats are meatless for the most part, containing various combinations of green vegetables, sunflower seeds, grain, natural honey, alfalfa, and other assortments of dehydrated vegetables.

## Hoarding

People like hamsters as pets for a number of reasons, one of which is the interesting way the animal stuffs his cheek pouches with food and then scurries away to hoard it.

*Hamsters stuff food in their cheek pouches and hoard it to eat later. Extra bedding will give your hamster a place to store his snacks.*

## Water is Essential

It is vital that your hamster be provided with a constant supply of fresh, clean drinking water every day. Water should be placed in a hanging water bottle and attached to the hamster's cage. Make sure the bottle doesn't leak or spill. Whenever you add or change the hamster's water, check the water bottle to see if it is working properly. Most water bottles are sturdy enough to withstand the hamster's gnawing, especially ones with metal sipping tubes. Never use a water bottle with a glass sipping tube, as your hamster can easily break the glass and become injured.

The hamster doesn't overeat. (You can, however, put too much weight on him by feeding him too many things from the family dinner or breakfast table.) Whether you feed him once a day at a set time, or simply refill his food supply when it starts getting low, you will find that your hamster will eat when he wants to eat, and he will hide the rest away to nibble on when he's hungry again.

Hamsters have different hoarding styles. A female hamster expecting a litter is a particularly busy hoarder. A nervous hamster or one who has been moved around a lot recently will stuff his pouches until he looks like some strange pet from another planet.

Most hamsters try to keep their hoard in one place in the cage, usually somewhere near where they sleep and as far away as possible from where they make their toilet. Always make sure that the cage has been furnished with enough bedding not only for sleeping and toilet areas but for food hoarding "kitchens" as well.

## Chewing and Gnawing

Gnawing sticks not only have a coating of tasty ingredients and seeds, but they also help keep the hamster's teeth trim and healthy; when the seeds are gone, the remaining wooden center is a good gnawing stick. Guinea pigs, mice, rabbits, gerbils, and hamsters all have teeth that grow constantly during their life.

This continuous growth must be worn away by gnawing before the teeth get too long. Overgrown teeth can lead to an inability to chew properly. Hamsters can develop lesions and sores because of overgrown teeth.

The vital importance of keeping their teeth in perfect shape helps to explain why hamsters are always gnawing on things. A hamster will chew on his cage, the metal end of a water bottle, food dishes, and whatever else he can get his teeth into—in the cage or out of the cage. To keep his teeth in shape and to keep the damage he can cause to a minimum, provide a good variety of gnawing aids in food and non-food form.

*Hamsters are known to play in their food dishes. Feed your hamster dry pellets in a heavy ceramic bowl, but provide fresh water in a hanging water bottle.*

## Food and Water Dishes

You should have two heavy, ceramic food dishes for your hamster. One will be used to feed him pelleted dry food, the other can be used for fresh fruits and vegetables. In addition to the weighted food dishes, the hamster's cage should have a water bottle attached to it. Don't use a water dish, as it may become contaminated with fecal matter or bedding. A gravity-fed hanging water bottle helps keep things clean and dry in the cage. The hamster will not be able to knock it over or spill the water into the bedding. Make sure to hang the bottle low enough so that your hamster can easily reach it to get water. Always check water levels to make sure that the water bottle is working properly and provide a fresh supply of cool, clean drinking water every day. You can find an assortment of food dishes and water bottles at any pet store.

## When and How Much to Feed

It's best to feed your hamster in the late afternoon or evening, which coincides with the natural activity level of these pets. It is important to feed your hamster at the same time each day. Provide him with a food dish of hamster food pellets and a small portion of fruit or vegetables that you know he likes.

There is no science of how much to feed your hamster, as different animals have different appetites. Many factors can contribute to how much of an appetite your hamster has, these include:

### An Easy Feed

Once you get in the habit of feeding your hamster, you won't even notice the time it takes. Choose a convenient time to feed your pet, such as the late afternoon or early evening. Make sure to feed your hamster at the same time every day.

*Offer your hamster a variety of fresh fruits and vegetables, such as apples, carrots, and broccoli. Be sure to wash all fresh foods before feeding them to your pet.*

1. Age of the hamster—A young, growing pet will eat more than an older, mature hamster.

2. Temperature of the hamster's environment—The warmer it is, the less the pet will eat because he does not need extra layers of fat.

3. Activity level—A hamster that has ample room for exercise will consume more food than one kept in small accommodations.

4. State of health—A fit hamster will have a larger appetite than one that is not feeling very well.

5. Breeding state—A breeding female will require progressively more food than will a non-breeding female.

Feeding Your Hamster

# What Do Hamsters Like To Eat?

Hamsters eat rolled oats, buckwheat, filberts, peanuts (a very good source of the important vitamin E requirement), sunflower seeds, corn, and wheat germ. Some hamsters might like certain foods more than others. Try out a few different treats and see which ones your pet prefers.

Hamsters like a variety of fruits and vegetables. Some favorites include: apples, plums, grapes, strawberries, bananas, carrots, celery, spinach, pears, broccoli, carrots, cauliflower (outside leaves and stalk), turnips, chicory, parsley, and cabbage and lettuce in small amounts. Feed another type of lettuce besides iceburg, as it is mostly water and has very little nutritional value.

Wild plants can be given as well. Examples are dandelion, chickweed, clover, and plantain. Never feed plants that are grown from bulbs, or any other plant that you are unsure of. If in doubt, leave it out.

6. Quality of food—The better the quality, the less will be consumed, as the better foods will be richer in their content.

Keeping all of these factors in mind, the best way to establish individual needs is by trial and error. Put a handful of dried foods into your pet's dish and see how much is consumed at a single sitting. Do likewise with a selection of moist foods. Adjust the next meal up or down according to whether or not any food was left. As a guide, there should be some dried foods left; but you do not want moist foods left out more than a couple of hours, or they will start to sour. This is especially true in warm weather.

It is important to remember that hamsters fill their cheek pouches with food and take it to their nest box to eat later. Check the nest box every two to three days to see how much, if any, food has been stored.

You should always watch your pet when he eats so that you know which foods are the preferred items. They are the ones that will be consumed first, so an order of preference can be determined.

If you want to try a new brand of pellets or experiment with a new fruit or vegetable, introduce the new food item gradually. Try mixing some of the old food pellets with the new until you have a good blend. Don't offer your hamster a huge portion of a new fruit or vegetable; give him a tiny portion to start, to see if he likes it and to avoid upsetting his stomach.

## Mineral Blocks

Vitamins are important to the well-being of hamsters. A vitamin deficiency can result in nervousness, inactivity, loss of hair, weight

*Sunflower seeds, grain, rolled oats, corn, and alfalfa make good dietary supplements or can be offered as treats. Give your hamster a variety to see what he prefers.*

*If you are providing your hamster with a balanced diet containing dry pellets and fresh foods, vitamin and mineral supplements will not be necessary.*

loss, and other problems. Vitamins also help to bring out the soft, lustrous beauty of the animal's fur. And, of course, vitamins also help to ensure that your pet gets all the vital nutrients that he needs. Vitamin E is particularly important for the hamster.

Food items, such as commercially-made "lickstones," provide salt and trace elements of zinc, manganese, iron, copper, iodine, and cobalt. The lickstone is a round spool that can be hung from the wires of the hamster's cage.

A mineral block is also a source of all of the elements found in the lickstone. The stone or mineral block is larger than the lickstone and should be placed somewhere on the floor of the cage. The block provides another outlet for the hamster to wear down his teeth safely. Such items are available at your local pet shop.

*A well-balanced diet will keep your hamster healthy throughout his lifetime.*

Feeding Your Hamster

## Vitamin Supplements

Vitamins are not really foods but chemical compounds that are crucial to good health. They enable chemical reactions within body cells to take place. There are a number of vitamins, some of which can be synthesized in the body, and some of which cannot and must be provided in the diet. If your pet eats a wide-ranging diet, then he is unlikely to ever suffer from vitaminosis, which is a lack of one or more important vitamins.

The reverse of this is hypervitaminosis, meaning an excess of these compounds. This is as dangerous as a lack of vitamins, so only provide vitamin supplements if your pet eats a very restricted diet, and then only under veterinary recommendation. Vitamin-rich foods include fruits, green plants and certain vegetables, fish-liver oils, and wheat germ. Each of these contains differing quantities of given vitamins, as do all foods.

Minerals are natural elements such as iron, copper, magnesium, potassium, phosphorus, selenium, and calcium. Lack of minerals can result in poor cell structure and problems in normal body functions. An excess of some minerals can disrupt the absorption of other minerals as well as the absorption of vitamins. However, these extremes are unlikely in a hamster that eats a typical well-balanced diet.

# Handling & Training Your Hamster

Because he is a caged animal, many people might think that a hamster should simply be left in his cage and given attention at feeding time. This is not the case. Hamsters should be handled frequently. It is important that your hamster is handled gently on a day-to-day basis. This way, he will become very tame and a joy to own. If he was a youngster when purchased, he should already be familiar with being picked up.

You should handle your pet hamster in order to build up a "relationship"; the more you handle the hamster, the more familiar he will become with you, the more he will trust and respond to you, and the better pet he will be. Hamsters will

## Hamster Handling

When handling your pet, don't put your hand over the hamster because you may frighten him. Hamsters are naturally friendly creatures and they will be friendly and curious as long as they are not startled. More often than not, bites from a hamster are caused by careless handling of the animal, or sometimes by movements on your part that are too fast for him to follow. A startled hamster may bite at a hand suddenly hovering over him.

become tame in a short period of time. Of course, before you start to handle or "hand tame" your hamster, you should learn the correct way to hold him. Remember that a hamster is quick, moves around a lot, and is sometimes hard to "get a handle on," but there are correct ways to handle him. Incorrect handling will only frighten and possibly injure your pet.

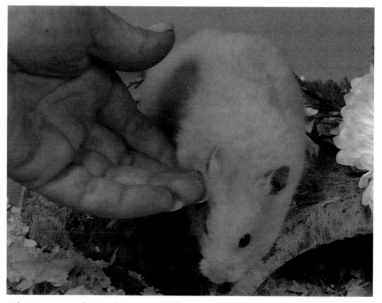

*Always approach your hamster slowly when you try to pick him up. Do not make sudden moves or startle your pet.*

*Teach children the proper way to pick up and hold a hamster. Talk calmly to your pet and he will become accustomed to the sound of your voice.*

Try to find time to play with your hamster during his normal waking hours—this will be in the evening and at night. If you do choose to spend time with your hamster during the daylight hours, be sure to wake him up gently and keep him out of any bright light. Let him awaken fully and then let him get used to you.

When you are petting or handling the animal, always let him know that you are there before you even attempt to pick him up. Pet him while he's still in the cage and let him get used to your hand by sniffing or exploring. You may want to offer a small treat or piece of food to entice him into your hand. Remember that your hamster is, by nature, a gentle, friendly pet and that you too must be gentle and friendly and patient. Patience is very important. If you try to hurry

*Handle your hamster every day, and in time and with patience, he will become a more sociable and friendlier pet.*

things, you will only frighten him and you both will have to start all over again.

You should always be gentle when waking and handling the hamster, and you should always proceed slowly. Let him gradually get used to you, to the sound of your voice, to the human smell of your hand. You want to reach a point where the hamster will respond to you and come to you on his own. Offer your hand slowly, giving him plenty of time to identify you as a friend rather than as an enemy. If your pet is unusually jumpy, it might be best to start by offering him the back of your hand rather than easily bitten fingers.

To make a hamster very friendly, you've got to spend a lot of time with him and handle him regularly. A new pet requires careful handling to build up trust, and that trust will increase. Like all animals, hamsters will bite, but there is less chance of that happening if they are handled regularly when they are young.

When picking up your hamster, try to cup your hands under and then over him so that he feels secure. Try not to be nervous or afraid

## Handling Food

It's not a good idea to handle your hamster after you've been eating or handling food. Hamsters rely on their strong sense of smell to find food. If you just finished eating a pear, he may smell the pear on your hand and take a bite. As a general rule, always wash your hands before handling your hamster.

because hamsters can detect this fear with their keen sense of smell and become nervous. Calmly talk to your hamster while you are taming it. The soothing sound of your voice will relax him and he will get to recognize your voice.

Always give your pet support from below. You may feel more comfortable holding him in hands clasped beneath him and thumbs forming a kind of roof over his head. Allow the hamster to walk into your handmade "cave" and then gradually, but not too gradually, tighten them around him. Do not hold him too tightly or squeeze him, as he will become frightened. Hamsters are fragile, and the spine should be protected from any unnecessary twisting or bending.

*One way to train or hand-tame your hamster is to offer him a treat to coax him to you.*

Before long, your hamster will become used to handling, especially if you spend time holding him every day. In time he will walk onto your hand or perhaps even crawl up your arm or sit calmly in your lap. Use common sense when you are handling or playing with the hamster. Never leave him alone and unsupervised while he is out of the cage. Be sure an adult is present if a young, inexperienced child is handling the hamster. Make sure that there is nothing around that the animal can fall on and injure himself.

## Taming Your Hamster

Taming is a more sophisticated aspect of pet handling. While the objective of correctly handling the hamster is for you to help the animal get used to you and not bite, the objective of taming is to make the animal friendly. Handling him will eventually lead to a point where he will trust you.

As is often the case in any part of the animal world, one of the keys to the taming of the hamster is in the ritual of "breaking bread" with the animal. In other words, you can break the ice and build up friendship with him a lot more easily if you have a hamster snack or treat to offer.

Taming, in our sense of the word, implies creating a working relationship between the pet owner and the pet to make everything easier, whether it's feeding, health care, maintenance of the cage, or just everyday contact. You want to develop a rapport with your pet so that you can work as a team to get things done. One of the things to accomplish is a spirit of cooperation. You can reach a point where you'll have the hamster voluntarily eating out of your hand.

# Hamster Health Care

With the right kind of care, hamsters should not get sick during their short life spans because they are naturally hardy and naturally resistant to disease and illness. However, they are also victimized by the same types of ailments that plague humans, and for some of the same reasons. They don't usually get sick, but if they do, it will probably be with the common cold and other upper respiratory maladies.

The best thing you can do to keep your hamster healthy is to practice a little bit of preventive medicine. To prevent the hamster from catching cold, make sure that the cage is situated away from all drafts. In the winter, during extremely cold spells you might want to add an extra layer of insulation under the animal's cage, and maybe even want to put a blanket over the top of the cage. Make sure, however, that the hamster won't be able to chew on it, and that the blanket doesn't stop the proper air circulation. In the summertime, make certain that the hamster isn't too close to air conditioning vents or fans.

Hamsters are hardy little pets, but there are many problems and diseases that they can suffer from if their living conditions are allowed to deteriorate, if their nutrition is inadequate, or if you are not careful and inadvertently expose them to pathogens (disease-causing organisms). Taking these factors into consideration, as a responsible pet owner, your priorities are to:

1. Avoid problems and disease by following correct husbandry techniques.
2. Recognize a hamster that is sick.
3. Take appropriate measures to isolate the ill pet.
4. Diagnose the problem.
5. Treat the hamster.

*Most health problems can be avoided if you keep your hamster's cage clean.*

## Recognizing an Ill Hamster

It is possible that an ill pet will display no physical evidence of a problem until he dies. However, he may exhibit changes in his normal behavior patterns. You can pick up on these only if you have spent time observing your pet.

Changes to look for are: disinterest in food or water, especially if this extends to known favored items; excessive sleeping during periods when the hamster is normally quite active; sluggish movements and general lethargy; aggression in a normally docile individual when being handled; excessive scratching or biting of the fur; ruffled or unkempt fur, uncoordinated body movements – such as fits; and excessive thirst. Any of these conditions are abnormal and do not occur unless there is a problem. If your hamster is displaying any of these symptoms, consult your veterinarian.

## Avoiding Problems and General Hygiene

Although it may seem an overworked remark, the fact is that general hygiene really does make the difference between having many health-related problems and having few, if any. More diseases are transmitted due to lack of hygiene than via any other source, so let us recap what your husbandry priorities should be.

1. Clean the hamster's cage every week. Do not forget the cage bars because your pet will often rub his snout on them, or gnaw on them.

2. Clean food bowls and the water bottle every day.

3. Store all dry foods in a cool, dry, darkened cupboard that cannot be contaminated by mice. Store fresh foods in the refrigerator. Never feed any stale foods and always remove uneaten fresh foods within an hour or so.

*Observe your hamster every day. An ill hamster may appear lethargic or stop eating.*

4. Wash your hands before and after handling your hamster. Always handle sick pets after you have completed your daily chores for other pets, and wash your hands after handling any potentially ill hamster.

5. Maintain a constant temperature (within 2 to 4 degrees) in the room where your pet lives. The preferred range for hamsters is 65°-80°F (18°-26°C).

Once you have determined that your pet is ill, you must not wait to see how things develop. Lost time can be fatal to a small animal like a hamster, which has a rapid metabolic rate. However, a fast metabolism also means that such animals can make quite dramatic improvements in a short time if treatments are prompt and appropriate. Make notes on the clinical signs that your hamster is exhibiting. Note the state of his fecal matter if possible, and obtain a specimen for your vet to examine if required. Note the progression rate of the illness. Take your hamster to the vet as soon as possible.

If you cannot get to the vet right away, take the following measures. First, isolate the pet away from other small animals. Raise the ambient temperature to about 90°F. This may overcome minor chill-related problems. It can be 2 to 4 degrees higher, but the danger in small, restricted cages is that the hamster may suffer from heat stress over a prolonged period.

If the pet's fecal matter is liquid, you should withhold moist foods (especially plant matter) until you can contact your vet. This will encourage the hamster to drink more water, which may be one of the ways in which a treatment may best be administered. Do not withhold water from your hamster, as this will make him dehydrated. Remember that when any animal has received short- or long-term heat treatment, it must be carefully acclimatized back to the temperature that it is normally accustomed to. The temperature should be reduced 1 to 2 degrees per day until it is at the normal heat level.

There are many drugs now available for the treatment of small mammals, and it is also possible to conduct surgery on these pets.

## Don't Play Vet

Home diagnosis of anything but minor problems is fraught with danger. Many of the clinical signs of ill health are the same for a whole range of diseases, but the treatments for them can differ considerably. If the diagnosis is not accurate, then it is not possible to prescribe a course of treatment. Often, microscopy of a blood sample, fecal matter, or a skin scraping is needed. Only your vet can attend to this need and provide the correct diagnosis to your hamster. It should be mentioned that penicillin is known to be dangerous to hamsters, as are a number of other antibiotics. The unqualified use of them is not advised.

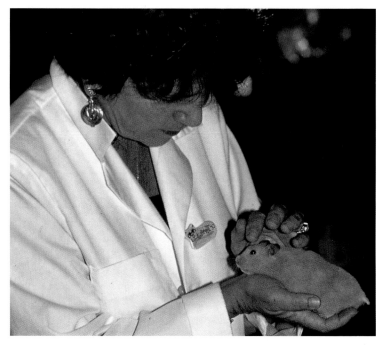

*If you suspect your hamster is sick, do not waste time trying to diagnose the problem yourself. Take your pet to the vet.*

Whether either of these modes of treatment is cost-justifiable can only be determined after consultation with your vet in light of the diagnosis. Medicine can be administered orally, by injection, or in the drinking water.

## Room Temperature and Hibernation

Always keep in mind that the hamster in your home is in a very different environment than his natural, native surroundings. In the desert, where the Syrian or Golden hamster is originally from, temperatures range from 100°F (38°C) and up during the day to the low 30s at night. However, in that environment, the hamster knows how and where to go to keep warm or cool. In man-made situations you have to help him out.

Moderation is the word when you're talking about the right room temperature for hamsters. Ideally, the Golden hamster should be put in a cage, in a room where the temperature is between 65° and 72°F (18°-22°C). Dwarf hamsters like it a little cooler.

Temperatures can drop below the 65°F (18°C) mark if the hamster's cage is furnished with an extra supply of bedding. This allows the animal to burrow or dig a little deeper and get extra warmth.

Of course, you don't want the temperature to drop too low (50°F (10°C) would be too low) because the hamster might not be able to burrow deep enough to get that extra warmth and he may go into a state of hibernation. He will sleep, his body will get rigid, and his body temperature will fall below normal.

Hamsters may hibernate under the following conditions: when the temperature drops below the normal range; when the hamster is able to store large quantities of food; when he is housed in deep litter that is not replaced on a regular basis; and when the pet is infrequently handled. When the hamster is in a torpid state, you may think that the pet has died or is seriously ill. But if your pet does become exposed to a major drop in temperature, you should slowly return the heat level a few degrees each day until activity is restored.

*Overall, hamsters are healthy pets that rarely become ill. A healthy hamster appears lively and alert and has a good appetite.*

## Hamster Illnesses
### Wet Tail

Wet tail is one of the most destructive diseases that a hamster can get. There are several theories on the causes of wet tail, none are absolutely conclusive, but one contributing factor in the disease and in the spread of the disease may be a build-up of dampness and humidity in the hamster's environment.

Some say that wet tail can occur after shipping or when hamsters have been crowded together too long in an inadequate cage. Overheating may also contribute to the problem because heat allows the infectious germs to multiply rapidly at a time when the animals are most susceptible to the germs.

Wet tail is also very contagious and can be spread by contaminated water from one hamster to the next. It can also be spread by simple contact. The symptoms are much the same as diarrhea, only much more severe. Hamsters hit with this disease must be treated immediately if they are going to have any chance of making it through. The main killer in the disease is dehydration due to diarrhea. To combat this, fluids must be readily available and within easy reach of the afflicted one, who, if struck by wet tail, will become emaciated and weak as the backside area gets wet and discolored.

Do all that you can do to prevent this disease. Besides keeping the cage clean and dry, make sure the bedding in the cage is dry from the surface to the bottom of the cage. This, however, poses still another problem in the entire wet tail dilemma. You are supposed to keep the hamster's cage as clean and dry as possible, but you have to do it in such a way that you won't upset the inhabitant. If you move things around too much or too often, you could cause the hamster to experience a certain amount of stress.

If wet tail does become a problem for your hamster, you should thoroughly clean and disinfect his entire cage, including the frame, the feeding dishes and bottles, toys, exercise wheel, and anything else of his or yours in the surrounding area in order to slow the spread of the disease immediately. Consider throwing away some of these items and getting new dishes, water bottles, and gnawing sticks. Of course, you must destroy old litter, bedding, and food,

*Wet tail is a serious disease that can be fatal to your hamster. It may be caused by crowded or damp living conditions. Keeping your hamster's cage clean helps prevent illnesses.*

# Stress

One theory views stress as a contributing factor in a hamster's succumbing to wet tail. This stress can be caused by a number of things, including excessive cleaning and disruption of the animal's cage or it can result from the hamster's inability to adjust to a new home. Any animal would be nervous at first in a new home, and an unlucky hamster might find himself in a home where children are always grabbing him, picking him up and dropping him, making loud noises and frightening him, turning on lights that are too bright, bringing in other animals, opening windows that allow too much cold air to enter, etc. Always treat your hamster gently and try not to contribute to any stress-causing factors.

and put new shavings, fresh food, and water in the cage after it has been thoroughly disinfected.

## Stomach Upset

If hamsters are exposed to food that has spoiled, intestinal problems may result. You can usually tell by the hamster's stool how healthy he is. Normal, solid droppings indicate that all is well. If his stomach is upset or if he is afflicted with other, more serious maladies, the droppings will likely be loose and watery. This could indicate anything minor (too many fruits and vegetables or ingestion of spoiled foods) to the more serious intestinal disorders.

## Abscesses

Abscesses are pockets of infection that can be caused by cuts or scrapes in the skin. Abscesses generally appear to be a lump under the skin and require veterinary attention so they can be drained and treated with hamster-safe antibiotics.

Conversely, the hamster may also suffer from constipation. Constipation in young or adult hamsters can result from too many dry pellets and not enough water. If you give your hamster dry pellets, you must provide plenty of fresh drinking water. In case of constipation, give young hamsters some greens and give adult hamsters carrots, leafy vegetables, and fruit.

Intestinal problems can develop when water is offered to the hamster in an open dish instead of in a standard water bottle. He might accidentally contaminate his drinking water with feces or rotting food. When contaminated water is consumed, many of the symptoms are similar to the intestinal problems related to food spoilage.

Diarrhea is also a common problem developed during shipping of hamsters, so it would be very wise for you to completely look over

*Stress can be caused by loud noises, drafts or chills, or can arise when the hamster is moved to a new home. Do all you can to keep your hamster comfortable and stress-free.*

Hamster Health Care

your animal in the pet store and to make sure he is healthy before you bring him home. Always check for signs of diarrhea and staining; if these are present, it is not a good idea to move the animal until the problem has been corrected.

## Colds and Respiratory Problems

The symptoms of a cold are inactivity and ruffled fur; the hamster's nose might look a little swollen, too, because he may be constantly wiping the nasal discharge on his fur. He may also sniffle and sneeze, lose a little weight, and lose a little luster on his coat. Loss of weight and ruffled coat are usually signs that something is wrong.

Ruffled coat, loss of appetite, rapid breathing, nasal discharge, coughing and sneezing could also be signs of more severe respiratory problems and the onset of pneumonia. Respiratory problems can develop in malnourished groups of damp and/or overcrowded animals. Poor air circulation could be another contributing factor.

*Your hamster relies on you to provide the best possible care you can. Take good care of your pet throughout his lifetime.*

# Fleas and Mites

Skin parasites are not common on pet hamsters, but if they do infest yours, there's a good chance that he got them from another household pet, such as a cat or dog; since both are more susceptible to the attack of fleas, lice, ticks, and mites.

If you have other animals in the house, the best thing to do for the well being of all your pets is to control parasites by using medications in spray or powder form. If you have a dog or a cat with a bad case of fleas, you should take him to a veterinarian or animal-grooming specialist and have the pests removed with a special dip before they go from your pets to the furniture and the rest of the house and reach the hamster's cage. Fortunately, there are good flea and lice treatments available from your vet. Repeat treatments will normally be needed to kill unhatched eggs that survive the first treatment. All hamster bedding and floor coverings must be destroyed and replaced if your pet gets fleas or lice. Be sure to inspect your pet on a regular basis for external parasites.

Preventing the development of these and other conditions, and their consequences, is always the first thing to try to accomplish with respect to hamster health care. If, however, the animal does come down with something and treatment is necessary, treat colds and sniffles with plenty of fresh food, clean water, a clean, dry cage and warm, soft bedding.

Sometimes there may be false alarms. For example, after the hamster has packed away one two many pellets in his cheek pouches, his eyes may start to tear, and it may look like he's starting to get a cold. This could simply be owing to the fact that some food has stuck in one of the animal's cheek pouches. To get excess food out of the cheek pouches, try using a medicine dropper filled with warm water to flush out the debris in the pouches.

## Wounds

If you notice your hamster has a small cut or wound, you should carefully clean the injury with tepid water. A hamster can reach his cuts and wounds with his tongue, and his constant licking of the wound will normally keep it from getting infected. If the cut or wound doesn't seem to be getting any better, treat it with an antiseptic applied with a cotton swab. A veterinarian should look at more serious cuts and wounds as soon as possible because an infection from the open wound may result.

## Household Pests

Contact with contaminated animals can be fatal to your hamster. You must do your part to make sure that wild rats or mice cannot get near your hamster's cage because they are carriers of a host of other parasitical diseases.

Household pests like roaches, bedbugs, and mites can sometimes get into hamster cages, especially in regions where there is a lot of heat

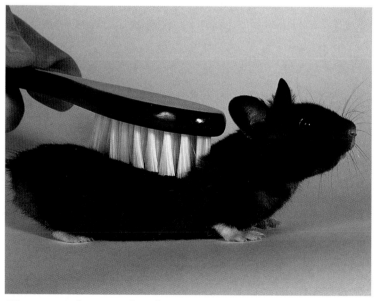

*Hamsters are clean animals and require little or no grooming. You can gently brush your hamster to comb out any loose hairs.*

## Grooming

Pet owners like the fact that the hamster is a clean animal. He cleans himself all day, licking his paws to wash his face. He uses his paws and tongue to clean his belly, back, and legs. The bath that the hamster gives himself, from head to toe, also serves to keep his coat clean and shiny. Therefore, unless he gets into a real mess, he should not require a traditional soap and water bath.

You might see the hamster preening the fur around the tiny gland he has on each hip. These glands secrete small quantities of a fluid something like musk. It does not mean that anything is wrong if he is spending a lot of time preening the fur around this gland. If you wish to brush your hamster, you can use a soft-bristled toothbrush to comb out any loose hairs.

and humidity. Get rid of them. Use insecticides, if necessary, but when doing so, remove the hamster from his cage and put him in a temporary home. (You might want to keep a small animal pen around the house for these and other emergencies.) Put the hamster in his temporary home and take him to another room, away from the noxious chemicals you are using. Disinfect the cage thoroughly, get rid of all old litter, food, water, and chewing sticks and replace them with new ones. Thoroughly clean the hamster's toys, the exercise wheel, and the tubes and slides in the cage. If your hamster playground is an intricately designed system, you will have to take it apart and give every nook and cranny a thorough cleaning.

If the problem is serious, you might even want to put the cage out in the fresh air to aerate it completely. While you are doing this, don't forget to clean the room the hamster usually lives in. Open all the windows to get rid of the chemical toxins in the air after the pest problem has been eliminated. Return the cage to the room and the hamster to his cage only when you are sure that everything is perfectly insect-free, clean, and dry again.

While bacteria, viruses, and disease can be transmitted to hamsters from other animals, you too, as owner of several pets, could also be a transmitter of bacteria and disease to your hamster. Always wash your hands before as well as after you handle your pet.

Hamsters that are well cared for, handled properly and fed nutritionally balanced meals, and whose cages are kept clean and dry, may live up to or a bit longer than 1,000 days. Toward the end of his life, the hamster may start eating less and start sleeping more. If he seems to be comfortable and is not suffering from any pain, he should be allowed to live out his natural life in his cage. Treat him gently and feed him whatever he will eat. If, however, your hamster has developed a condition that makes him uncomfortable and causes him to experience pain, the humane thing to do is have your veterinarian evaluate his quality of life and make the best decision for your pet's well-being.

# Resources

### American Hamster Association
Attn: Membership
PO Box 457
Leavenworth, KS 66048
http://www.joinAHA.org

### California Hamster Association
23651 Dune Mear
Lake Forest, CA 92630
Email: calhamassoc@hotmail.com
www.geocities.com/CalHamAssoc/

### The Hamster Club of America
New Memberships
PO Box 27862
Santa Ana, CA 92799-7862
Chat room: http://hca.hyper-mart.net/chat.html

### HamsterLand
Website with everything you need to know about caring for your hamster!
http://www.HamsterLand.com

### The Hamster Society (UK)
Membership Secretary
The Hamster Society
3 Laverockdale Loan
Edinburgh EH13 0EZ
Scotland
www.forrestg.pwp.blueyonder.co.uk/hamsoc/

### Pioneer Rat and Hamster Society (PRHS)
PO Box 10624
Kansas City, MO 64188-0624
http://www.prhs.info

### Rat, Mouse and Hamster Fanciers
2309 Country Ranch Drive
Modesto, CA 95335
Email: jstarkey@telis.org
http://www.ratmousehamster.com

# Index

## Photo Credits

*Joan Balzarini: pp. 38, 44, 52*
*Isabelle Francais: pp. 1, 4, 7, 33, 35, 39, 41-43*
*M. Gilroy: pp. 3, 8, 9, 11, 18, 20, 25, 29, 45, 53, 57*
*Andre Roth: p. 47*
*Vince Serbin: pp. 5, 37, 58*
*Laura Stern: p. 60*
*John Tyson: pp. 13, 14, 17, 22, 27, 31, 48, 50, 55*

Quick and Easy Hamster Care